Big Water

Books by John Engels

The Homer Mitchell Place   1968
Signals from the Safety Coffin   1975
Blood Mountain   1977
Vivaldi in Early Fall   1981
Weather-Fear: New & Selected Poems   1983
The Seasons in Vermont   1983
Cardinals in the Ice Age   1987
Walking to Cootehill: New & Selected Poems   1993
Big Water   1995

Big Water

Poems
by
John Engels

Afterword
by
David Huddle

Artwork
by
Alan James Robinson

Lyons & Burford, Publishers

Printed in the United States of America

Designed and composed by Trade Composition

10 9 8 7 6 5 4 3 2 1

Engels, John.
    Big water / John Engels.
        p.   cm.
    ISBN 1-55821-357-0. — ISBN 1-55821-358-9 (pbk.)
    1. Fishing—Vermont—Poetry.   I. Title.
PS3555.N42B54   1995
811'.54—dc20   94-30963
                                                          CIP

ACKNOWLEDGMENTS

"Rainbows False-Spawning" first appeared in *The Reporter*, and was collected in *The Homer Mitchell Place* (Pittsburgh: University of Pittsburgh Press, 1968)

"An Angler's *vade mecum*" appeared in earlier versions in *Atlantic Salmon Journal* and *Random Casts*, and was collected in *Signals From the Safety Coffin*, (Pittsburgh: University of Pittsburgh Press, 1975). The poem is based on the tone and language of certain testimonial letters that appeared in *Hardy's Angler's Guide: Coronation Issue of 1937*.

"Mudtrapped," appeared in *Vivaldi in Early Fall* (Athens: University of Georgia Press, 1981)

"Dead Pool" first appeared in *The American Fly Fisher*, and was collected in *Weather-Fear: New & Selected Poems, 1958–1982* (Athens: University of Georgia Press, 1983)

Parts of "Thunder River" appeared in *Trout* (Autumn 1988) in another form.

"Gutting Bluefish" (under another title), "The Storm," "Pilgrimage," "Foote Brook," "At Night on the Lake in the Eye of the Hunter," "The Marshes at Suamico, Wisconsin," "Damselfly, Trout, Heron," "Bullhead," "Muskrat," "The Raft," "Photograph," "Crows," "The Guardian of the Lakes at Notre Dame" and "East Middlebury" appeared in *Walking to Cootehill: New & Selected Poems, 1958–1993*, and are reprinted by permission of the University Press of New England.

"Big Water" and "The North Branch" appeared in *Gray's Sporting Journal* (March 1994 and March 1995 respectively)

"A Fly Box," "Letter," "Green Bay Flies," "White Miller" and "Hatch" appeared in *New England Review*. (Winter 1994)

For Zimmer,
with love

Contents

Part II
The North Branch

Gutting Bluefish

Down on the shore
big black-winged gulls
slide in from nowhere
and swarm the bluefish guts
I've just flung onto the rocks,
gasp and mutter, and together

with the onshore wind
and the small surf, make
another voice, the only fit name for which

is laughter. And though it's early,
the sun barely clear of itself,
there's all this young light
on the verge of fire,

sea and sky reflected,
imagined and reimagined each
in the other so powerfully, I almost doubt

the prospect of darknesses
to follow, and so go on
trying to look to where
the sea has become
not clearly itself, to where
it continually vanishes
past the black headland

PART I

Looking for Water

Looking for Water

A river is supposed to be nearby, and reachable
and since in a strange place the first thing
is to look for running water, I ask, and discover
that no one knows exactly
where the river is, though
there's plenty of speculation,
they think it might be somewhere back below
where the hiking trails used to run,
beyond the old bridle paths, probably
overgrown by now, as they recall, a difficult

tangle of distance over steep descents
through grapevine, blackberry, alder hells.
I have to make my own way, following
in the hardening red clay the beautiful tridental tracks
of what turn out to be a dozen
wild turkeys that a scant ten yards ahead
take wing in the watery dusk,
flap up and glide back over the road, slow
as big, bronze, iridescent fish,
the whole time wind like a minor surf,
and while I'm still breathing hard, six deer
exactly the color of hickory startle and crash off
through a sudden general reddening of the day,
and staring after them I see
a white gleam through the trees,

not the river, but a headstone—I've come
on the old graveyard,
where the turkeys must just
have been feeding, and the deer
running through, leaping the headstones
of Cheatham and Goode, *Asleep
in Jesus,* and the Glasgow sisters, dead

at ten and two and eight,
reason enough to give up and head back.
and I'm home after dark
where a globed lamp in the farthest dip of the lawn
I mistake for the moon on water.

Rainbows False-Spawning

I'm amazed at what I see in the flat of the Falls Pool,
under an oblique sun, scarlet spasms of rainbows
finning over their marble redds
in false spawn—an April-breeding fish
in the flat of the year frenzied over stones, fins set
and flared, vermilion of gills—and October
paling in a milty haze, except for the maples,
orange as roe. I see again

the unseasonable pattern, fall skies
heavy as an April flood, a child in an instant
out of breath, a new-dropped Hereford lying
on snow in a steam of blood, October ludicrous
with color, red leaves in the bitter stream,
and here these fool fish spawn
in all and fierce conviction

under the maples where in August
spent flies eddied in yellow drifts,
and I heard the roaring of a million bees
among the sweet leaves like a wind.

Aquarium

I hadn't touched it for months,
the water had long cleared itself, the plants
flourished and thickened,
and at the end of my room
it seemed another room
pouring out light.
Daily the red oranda
came up for food, likewise
the bubble eye, ryunkin, black
dragon eye. But something began
to go wrong—quite suddenly
one of the buffaloheads, though desperate
to feed, could not swim up
from the bottom,
and the great calico veiltail as I watched
capsized, and swam upside down
no matter what I did

to the beautiful water, changed it, warmed it, cooled it,
measured out medicines
and salt, no matter how—
everything having failed,
and in the last extreme helpless—
I tried to cure it with light: dimmed

the aquarium, brightened it
to something like
morning, made it night again,
then morning again, then night. . . .

At Night on the River

When night comes in, wary
as a trout, ready in an instant
to shrink back
onto the kernel of darkness
from which it hatched
I've thought it might be worth dying
just to drown and be buried here.
You need to stand
to your knees in the Winooski at night all night
in wait for the back flow
of darkness, the river meantime

crushing waders onto skin, muscle, blood, bone.
Among other things you'll find
that at night the river smells sour and steely,
the air burns like a coin on the tongue,
that the river bears past
in driftlines
of light. Nothing is enough, something,
probably the tedious songs
with which we've tried
to replace ourselves have kept us
uneasy. But lean close
to the water. At night standing in the river
the name you spoke all day
will give way to another. You'll forget
to bear in mind how little
you'll resemble what you see.

MUDTRAPPED

One time I waded far out in a lily slough
on the Clyde's backwaters, and my boots
caught in powerful suctions of black ooze,

and I sank, until the water, at my chin,
stopped rising on me—something held me up.
I drank warm air, and well I might have stayed

forever there, deep-rooted in the bottom mucks
like some enormous lily. But my friends came.
I was rooted out, dragged in.

I've thought if it's true the black night sometimes
swallows us like that, the planet softens, liquefies,
tries to draw us in to where we drown,

it is the grace and rule of counterpoise applies—
or so Desire requires us to believe,
fearing as we do Love's natural buoyancies

are no true balance to the pulling-down.

FALLING IN

At my age gone awkward
having forgotten everything
I ought to have remembered
about keeping balance, I fall off the boat
trying to board the dinghy,
like in a Buster Keaton bit, the dinghy
skidding away and swamping and my legs

spreading, till in I go, and come up
kicking and sputtering, then find I can't
make it back into the boat, grab hold
of the high gunwale, and heave, but can't
get leverage, chin myself
a dozen times till I think
I've lost my breath for good, and end up
clinging to the rudder, exhausted, beginning to feel

the cold, the knowledge dawning
that I'm in trouble, big trouble. But I wait,
thinking something has to happen
to get me out of this, though I can't think
what it might be. But I'm wrong, nothing
happens, time

drags, and it's cold, it's cold,
too early to be swimming, too far to swim,
too deep to wade in, nothing happens and I try

waiting it out, but it goes on too long,
and nothing to do but after a long time
give up—whereupon I yell, holler,
bellow for help, loud
and bitterly ashamed. And after all

there's some guy working on his boat
who hears me and comes down
to the end of the dock and spots me
and rows out and saves me, and that's
the end of it. After he's gone,
I stand here on the dock,
dripping to a cold puddle
thinking it over, trying to name

how I'm feeling—not
relief, no remnant fear
or after-fear, but mainly
embarrassment, the tag-end
of something like boredom, a growing cold,
most of it left over from out there, and still growing,

but give it up and go out
to retrieve the dinghy, retrieve
some of the duffel, find one oar,
and a floating glove,
but I'm cold, and leave the rest
to drift in in its own time,
and all the way home, the cold
hanging on, my calves knotting

with cold, the world
ashiver, I begin
thinking to myself, *I'm
in trouble, this
is going to take
a long time, what do I do
until it's over?*

THE MARSHES AT SUAMICO, WISCONSIN

At the edge of the marshes the cattails leaped with frogs.
One of us found twined on a sedge a tiny green snake,
a vigor of grassy light burning its slow way out,
picked it up, let it coil on her palm,
wave its head, flicker its coral tongue—

carried it so for a while until it grew frightened,
tensed and gave off for so small a thing
a remarkable, high-flavored reek. She flung it away,
and none of us ever could find it again,
though we kept on the lookout. Then, deeper,

the marsh smell began, the air clean enough
until we stirred up the mud, slogging through
to the blinds, our trails filling in
with a fetid thickness of oozes, only the pale
swath of bent reeds to show how we'd come.

The lake leached in from beneath. Where we walked
was something less earth than water, swelling
with bubbles that burst through the duckweed and cress,
our faces at intervals swept with clean stony gusts
from the open lake. The mallows were springy

with redwings. Everywhere flashed green bolts
of dragonflies, snakes and turtles cruised
the channels, feathers of mud braided lakeward. At dawn
came the ducks, the sky awash to the feathery roots
of its undersoils—mallard and canvasback,

teal swung in to the blinds, or flared
on some sheen of the wind. In the marshes at Suamico,
watchful, we felt the world borne down
by its own abundances. Wherever we broke
through the pursy earth there billowed about us a quick

exhalation of soils, a rich recognizable stink,
while over us there in the dawn shone the bird-ridden sky.

Pilgrimage

On the night of the first killing frost
I come to the river through the cornfield
above Chapman's Cove, out of sight
of the cove's resident heron. I come every year
to watch the ground fog pour
in soft falls over the lip of the bank. I come
to the surge of the big water through a mist
of birches. The maples
drop their leaves, and the current
goes crimson, the pools and eddies
churning and frothing with color. I come to sit
on the big rock below the rapids, and find
once more that the October maples
on the river's far side seem
an impossible clarity of color, a dream
of color, I find
how exhaustible are the names
for color. Later on

I step into the stream,
and it's warmer than the air. I
begin to wade, the Winooski deepening
and rising on my upstream hip, the great
downbearing river beginning
to make itself dangerously felt, and then

and just in time past midstream
diminishing so that I come through
safe to the pale
minnowy shallows pull myself up
by the gray roots of a maple,
turn back and look out
over the whole dangerous power
of water translated
into a current of fog. I can't see
the far bank, and stand where I am
until it's wholly dark, afraid
to cross back, stand there
until the moon is fully risen
and the maples shine forth again
as if it were fully day, in the last
seasonal burst of the last
color, for which, on this night
of a killing frost, my breath
grown visible before me, I cannot
and do not wish to find a name.

FOOTE BROOK

At the foot of the slope down which
we faltered, the night roared, the brook
being in full spate. Unbalancing,
we leaned into pliancies of birch,

caught ourselves against
the pitchy hemlocks. Then,
before we'd quite expected it,
we breathed spray—

we were almost there. Because the moon
excited to light the edge of a cloud,
the brook at the falls leaped for an instant
with radiance, though elsewhere

light did not abound, nor would we
at that moment have said
night had by ordinary canon
come upon us. The brook was no more

than a minor brightness, yet its voice
was a powerful spasm of the night,
and the large world everywhere
so bountiful an irregularity of surfaces

we could scarcely keep our feet.

THE DISCONNECTIONS

When suddenly he took whom I had sought
in the endless trolling back and forth
off Cape Bianca *(froth of bonito*
boiling at sardines on the quarter, brake
and plunge of pelicans, off the bow
the huge cloud shadow of the manta, the stony sea
shattering on the Santa Helena reefs and then
the black fin trailing the rigged balao, *the cobalt bill*
thrusting up from the wake, the line
unclipping from the right outrigger,
running loose) I waited, and struck
into the living shock and weight of sea
and sailfish, and at the hookbite
the sheer silver of him leaped and leaped,
the great fin for an instant billowing
with purple light, and then
he broke away, the line end writhing
far astern, the big rod
springing back, whereupon
I reeled in and sat stunned, to imagine
his stunned and panicked seaward flight,
the snapped line snaking
at his flank; and remembered
what in fact had been too brief
in the true light of that afternoon
to have recollected with much

in the way of faith, except
for the usual conviction out of evidence—my hands
loosened on the rod, my heart
giving way a little, salt crystals
grainy on my lips, my wondering
how it might have been this time
to have brought him flaring and wallowing
in iridescences of spray boatside,
wide-gilled and azure, shimmering, gaffed him in
and lashed him down astern, swathed him
in damp sacking against the sun.

An Angler's *vade mecum*

1

Remember that the simplest eddy,
current and cross-current,
appall the fly. Remember also
that the fly should swim
as dun from nymph, and imago

from dun. Be aware
of season, of how trout go dull
and take on color with the trees.
Remember that the planet
trembles to a falling leaf
for trout. Therefore, be cautious

how you walk the riverbanks.

2

I have thought about it
often. I have thought of the salmon
as a difficult fish.
More than once

I've raised fierce shadows
from among the rocks,
and there is considerable art
to this—but it is best

to speak flatly in such
matters: the salmon
has eluded me. I fear
my shadow must have fallen
on the stream.

3

I cast to salmon with a rod
made of a lively cane, and nicely
fitted, the male ferrule
made to go

right home. Such tackle
promises success and pleasure,
while with a rod too soft
in its fibers, I should

be made too much aware
of the toothed hook
of the kype, the maniacal rush
downstream. I have

a *pâpièr* model
of a salmon. I am
pleased with it, it is
most natural. As a sportsman

and angler the exact
reproduction of natural
objects appeals
to me. It is

with great pleasure
that I possess
this reproduction, which looks
as if it were just out

of the water. I have not
taken salmon yet,
but perhaps in days ahead.
He is a spawning fish,

and does not feed.
Strong tackle
is required.

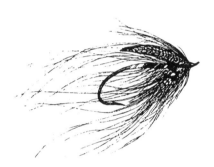

4

When, many years ago,
this rod was built, I took it
to the Miramichi, and everyone roared
at my using such a light stick

for such strong fish, and I recall
their amazement at my handling
of two grilse when fishing
for small trout, with midge flies

on a small river. Since then
it has killed thousands
of fish, and considering
the size of the rod, this seems

adequate performance.
And with it I can reach
well out into any river,
against any downstream wind

to the farthest rising fish
with no effort, and the strongest fish
has no chance of beating
me. I recall

one big and fresh-run salmon
took the line
under the canoe, and we
could not get it cleared, and this rod

before I knew it bent
clear round from the tip
to the center. The tip
was a little twisted, but

within an hour was back
to shape, being cut
from a lively wood.
I killed

three or four nice fish
right after that, and finished them
quickly, time being too dear
on a sporting stream

to waste much on a fish.
This rod will kill a trout
in a minute to each pound of weight,
and if with this rod I cannot

handle any fish as I please,
I know it is not the fault
of the rod, which is—I say it
freely, the most perfect

instrument I have ever
held in my hands.

5

Although I have used this rod
mainly for trout on small rivers,
it has been pressed into service
for tiger fish. A month ago

it landed an accidental
turtle. I am happy to say
that in spite of this
regrettable incident

its power and accuracy have been
in no way impaired.
And with this rod,
which was my father's

for thirty-five years before
it was mine, I took
a thirteen-pound salmon
in the Miramichi in eight

minutes. The water
was low, I walked back
onto the gravel, I reeled the fish
onto the gravel, my friend

timed the play of this fish.
A little later, when time decrees
I shall pass it on
to my son. I have

used it for thirty years myself,
mostly for trout
in small rivers. It is
an artist's rod, powerful

enough to kill heavy trout,
and yet it fishes so light
I have often lent it
to ladies. But I think

careful copies might be made
which might be just as good.

6

I enclose with this letter
a photograph of the salmon,
and the proud fisherman,
me. You can see

that the fish is better
than average for this stream.
I display him
from a hawthorn branch.

You can see
the harebells and cornflowers
that bloom from his gills:
my ghillie

put them there. It is
apparently a custom
in these parts. And I
am there, at left, attentive

to my kill, although
I am unsmiling, seriously staring
into the lens, for I wish not to seem
boastful, nor in any way

above my station, for this
is a kingly fish. My ghillie holds
my Hardy's celebrated
"Alnwick Greenheart,"

built suitable for salmon
trout and grayling, and he fiddles
with my reel, a brand-new
"Cascapedia." The river

eddies to a shore of daisies
in the background right. The rapids
of the pool are out of sight, but it was there
this great fish had tried to kill

a full-dressed Beauly Snow 3/0
blue-furred and tinseled, orange-headed
winged with peacock herl
that quartered flittering, across

his lie, a roar of color designed
to exasperate him, and it did,
to his lordly death.
But the biggest masterpiece

done by me was when I—
not with this but with another rod,
got a salmon in the Äaro River, in
Sögndal, in

Sögn. The weight
of this greater fish was
forty-three pounds, and I
was three hours

landing him, and you can bet
it was a strain on the rod,
but it was just as good
after as when

I began. I enclose
a second photograph of my
greater fish, and the proud fisherman,
me. The rod in this picture

was made from well-seasoned
greenheart, and my dear friend
for more than twenty-five
years. But now old age has claimed us.

DAMSELFLY, TROUT, HERON

The damselfly folds its wings
over its body when at rest. In the hand
it crushes easily
into a rosy slime.
Its powers of flight
are weak. The trout

feeds on the living damselfly—
the trout leaps from the water
and if there is sun you will see
the briefest shiver of gold,
then the river again.
When the trout dies
it turns its white belly
to the mirror of the sky.
The heron fishes for the trout

in the gravelly shallows
on the far side of the stream. The heron
is the exact blue of the shadows
the sun makes of trees on water.
When you hold the blue heron
most clearly in your eye,
you are least certain
it is there. When the blue heron dies
it lies beyond reach
on the far side of the river.

At Night on the Lake
in the Eye of the Hunter

That night, drifting far out
in the center of the lake, I watched
the stars; later,
I shone my torch down into the eelgrass
of the perch beds, and saw the fish
stunned into thrills
and tremblings of fins.

I shone the torch onto my wet hands,
the wet sky-reflecting floorboards
of the boat, onto the sky itself,
the beam widening and thinning
into the white fabrics of mist. That night

I thought I rode the center of all
the widening darknesses
to the rimstones of the encircling earth.
Later, by starlight seeing

over the whole blue surface of the lake
trout feeding on mayflies, seeing the cross
and recross of rise rings, the slow
opening ripples from the bright
tiny insucks at center,

I came to think how it might be
my boat hung there in a net of fire,
but however it was, the light
had begun its long reach, even now

long afterward, still rising,
widening into the body of the sky,
through the mists into the last
huge widenesses of the last
meetings of light beyond which
I remember this or not, beyond which
even then fearing my life
I wished to burn.

The Storm

I will myself not to despair
when I wait by the sea for good weather.
Even on the brightest of days
the storm has been a continual
awful hanging in the air,
and comes often, and endures,
longer each time, sometimes early

after a windless night that has been calm
with moon and stars, a fog
hanging low and close into the coast, soft
against the window, then
clearing, then

a line of big thunderheads advancing
from the north where last time
I happened to look nothing was, only
the broadest of daylight. And then
the sky breathes deeply,
and before I can think

the whirligig in the yard has spun itself
to pieces, the sea is shuddering
to its floor, and the sea
has flung itself at the window, the window
has bulged inward
and the beach plum and beach roses
have blown flat and seem about
to uproot and fly away,

and it is here, just at this spot
where America stops
thirty feet over the long, unhappy reach
of the ripped Atlantic, that this
is being written—in Maine
looking north from a streaked window
toward some black, savage rock of an island
I have never seen before and swear

wasn't there before,
and that seems at this very instant
to have at once fallen from the sky
and boiled up from below, and is being
devoured by its surf, and can be reached
only by swimming.

THE RAFT

His father told him to be careful,
to go no farther than the boundaries
of the lily cove. His father told him
once more about his cousin Archie

who had fallen into the scalding water
of the switchyard sump, because
the cinders floating between the tracks
had made it seem to be dry ground.

He wasn't thinking where he was,
he wasn't watching, he was thinking
of something else, his father said.
So he agreed he would watch

where he was going, wanting badly
to get down to the lake and out
to where the bottom
wasn't clear, to where

it was not evidently safe. *That day*
he never came home to eat, he never
came home, he was dead, and nobody
knew it, they just

went on with whatever it was
they were doing for themselves. His father
was going on and on like that
when he ran out the door and down

to the old dock, and found the raft
hidden in the reeds along the shore,
splintery pine boards scummy
with moss and mud. And when

he pushed it into the knee-deep water
at the end of the dock and stood, it ducked
and wavered and nearly heaved him off,
but held, an inch awash, instep-deep.

He sprawled down onto his belly
and paddled out with his hands,
like swimming—from up in the house
his father might have seen him

confidently swimming, headed out beyond
the boundaries, but in fact safe,
even should he range beyond the cove
to the dark line where the wind began—

though it was strange, even frightening,
to cup his hand around his eyes, lean
close to the surface, so that his nose
touched water, and look

through water and see
dense golden fields of weed. It was strange
to want so much to stand up on the raft,
step boldly off and walk

over the feathery tips of the weeds
to shore, his father watching, walk
straight up on shore, and call
to the terrified house

he was safe and had come back and the lake
had borne him up as he had known it would
and there had been from the first nothing
to worry about, nothing at all.

Staring down into the water, still bellied down
onto the raft, he saw
the skin of the lake thicken
with fiery clouds, because the sky

had thickened with fiery clouds,
so that there in the blazing lake,
in the pale cloud of his unwary face,
was the awful issue of the looking back.

THE PHOTOGRAPH

From the young birch lining the far shore
the crows called, erupted into the sky
out of the yellow leaves, flurried there,
fell back. The sun was high,

everything in perfect order on the raft,
the anchor rope in a tight spiral, weighed
by the scarlet coffee can half-filled
with cedar-smelling loam

from the swamp's edge. He spilled
a handful onto the rough pine
of the deck, threaded a worm, let it down,
careful it didn't snag, until the line

went slack, and he thought the lead
had touched bottom, drew it up a bit,
then waited, leaning over, trying to see
into the shadows among the twists

of pickerel weed, the light
where it touched the water going green,
slanting down into the weed beds, silvery
with dusts and pollens. Over the clean

sand bottom schools of yellow perch,
bluegill, redeye, lavender and flash
of shiners, waver and ripple of light,
short bursts of gold and green

where the young bass fed. But nothing
happened, nothing. He waited for a bite,
and when he looked up his eyes
dazzled at the sky. It was as if he still

were looking into water, for the sun
was low, and a green light rose
from among the cedars. His mother stood
on the beach and called, but he chose

not to hear, though she called and called.
At last he looked up and saw her there
farther off than he had thought,
her dress blowing, her feet in deep sand.

So he began to paddle back, the raft
wanting to turn in circles, the wind
opposing him. So he stood and leaned
into the paddle, dug hard, looked up again

and saw the beach was empty, the lake
ruffling, the water gone dense
and steely. It took him more time
than he'd thought he had to get back. It was not

as if truly he'd had a choice—the wind
had turned against him, and when
he stared into the water his face
did not look back. He felt the rain begin,

and while he struggled toward the beach
his mother came back and took a photograph
that caught the raft low down in the chop
seeming a powerful distance from shore,

and him, paddle in hand, the birch
on the far shore bristling up from the snowy sand,
everything badly overexposed—it frightened him to see
how far out on the lake he'd been.

He was frightened not to see
his face, but only a dark shape
under the hat brim. Even though
it had been in Klondike in St. Marie's General Store

where he'd stood to hold and see the photograph,
to his bare feet the plank floor solid, dry
and gritty, it hadn't been at all
certain that the foolish one in the photograph

wasn't slowly sinking into the lake, endangered
and alone, calling out to the mother who stood intent
her camera to her eye, framing him there,
catching the birches, the crows overhead,

the lake rising on him—somehow the fishy air
gathering, the sky gathering, around him
the deepening smell of cedar before rain,
the blue surge of lightning for the moment withheld.

A Photo of My Mother
and My Grandpa Lighting Out

Look at that, blood
to blood, my grandpa used to say,
at sunset or sunrise, *that's all it is, one's*
the back end of the other, take your pick. It's 1912,
July, after dawn, and they're looking to take
some brookies from the Little Beaver, lighting out
on his bike, in overlappings of fog
though underfoot

little brightnesses explode
from the flinty gravels,
likewise from the handlebar bell, the earpiece
of his glasses, what might be a ring
on my mother's hand. They're lighting out,

but posing too. It's so early in the morning,
my mother's thinking
the little trout must be asleep
just as she'd like to be,
that dew is still settling without brilliance
onto the cattails, and the redwings
haven't gotten around to being
awake yet, only an occasional dazed cheep
or whistle from the ditch, or from deep

in the marsh grass. Skunks
and raccoons must be still up and about, the sun
is the barest of reddenings over the spruce

from east of Joe's Island, and just beginning to pink
the first frettings of wind on Bawbeese Lake. The world's

fragrant—marsh mud and cedar, a faint
fishiness to the air, dust that smells like dust
one minute after rain. I get this, all of it
except for the color and the smells, which I'm obliged
to make up, sounds too: birds,
the scouring of bike wheels
over gravel. And one or two
small motions: dew falling, the tiny
surgings of grass, unfoldings
of violets, mallows, wild roses. I get all this
from the murky photograph, taken
too early in the morning, not near
enough light. My mother's young,
she's hanging on to my grandpa's checkered shirt
with one hand, with the other
a Prince Albert can which must
be full of worms, the old paper
is cracked across her face which she turns
to look back at someone
or other's camera. She's wearing

white stockings, high shoes, gray cloche, gray
gloves, my grandpa's got on
a boater, he's carrying the rods
across his handlebars, he's troubling
to keep upright and still
be slow enough for the Brownie's lens,
and the bike is listing, front wheel sharply

angled. Ahead of them the marsh
is a low gray hedge of shadow readying itself
for light, for birdsong, for a fullness of sun, for all
the various blossomings they probably expect—and that

is where they're going to, that
is where they're lighting out for,
ready to follow the long
slow leap of their shadows before them,
the night distending into dawn.
Therefore I hold the picture
at a certain angle to the sky

and my mother and my grandpa disappear
in a little square of light, a dull fire
that from somewhere deep
in the dimensionless old paper
has stirred, found fuel, surfaced, ignited.

THE CROWS

When it was spring in Wisconsin, and the roosting crows
screamed every morning from the birch grove
across the lake, alarmed
at the first predatory light,

I used to push out from shore
on my little waterlogged raft
awash to my ankles, and find it possible
to believe myself standing on still water
over the dangerous place
where the sand bottom dropped
into the muds of the spring hole.

When it was spring in Wisconsin, and morning,
the nights never far away, and the stars
preparing to burn in the rising field of the lake,
when it was spring and what I stood on
did not fully bear me up,
and if I could drown or fly or hurl myself
into the left and right of the powerful distances,

I had not sufficiently fathomed
how to believe, intent as I was
on the instance of morning, the voice
of the crow, small shivers of air
in the delicate drum of the bone, the rising
beaked sun. I'd stand on the lake
in the jaws of the opening light,

a deepening beneath me, a greater overhead,
the gesture of my reaching out to either side
a movement of so little extension I might,
but do not remember, have shouted

aloud and heard in reply
my own voice fly at me, back
from the trees of the far shore, the words
jumbled and raucous, prolonged
into warning, back
like the bright alarm
of the sun-greeting voices of crows.

The Guardian of the Lakes at Notre Dame

I can no longer bring to mind
the name of the ancient Brother
who patroled the lakes at Notre Dame
and ran us kids off, waving his old gun
from the far shore, shouting in a voice
that from a hundred yards away
seemed dangerous as a sword.

Retired to guard the lakes, the old man did.
For him to wake up was most powerfully to insist
that turtles be troubled merely to feed,
herons to fly, snakes to dream of toads.
Himself the caring center
of all careless natural grace, at last
he died. The lakes were fished.

There is something to be said
in favor of old men who raise the guardian arm and voice
against the hunting children—who, but lately come
to Paradise, pursue the precedent beasts
unto their dumb destruction, and persist.

Surely to him the sky came more and more to seem
like the dark-enclosing vault of the dead
box-turtle's shell. Perhaps he thought to cry
against us children was like love,

love being often in rebuke of innocence.
But as it went, we plundered the far shore,
and daily he waved his gun and shouted out at us

go home, go home! in fierce order that we might
be made to see how in the end the bellowing angel
raises up his fist, and how that is to be
forfeit of name in the memory of men.

East Middlebury

With small confidence in skill, tackle, gear,
years upstream of us, inattentive
and restless to renounce
everything we might have failed
to remember—on that day

of more than ordinarily dank sun,
thigh-deep in the familiar river
in which we no longer believed,
each of us pointed out to the other
where at the pool's head had occurred
one tiny rise—upon which came another,

more vigorous, and another, and so on, until
before long the river from bank to bank was lively
with splashes to a hatch
of little yellow mayflies,
which at this time of the afternoon at this time
of year, we ought to have
expected, and to which short and late
we cast, raising at once three
minor trout, then waded ashore to rest
in the strangeness it was to have undertaken

out of little hope the old rubric,
and by the agitations of the inert surface
to have been restartled.

DEAD POOL

Never in all my days on this stream
have I taken a trout from this pool
under the black willow—a good place
for big fish, the current deeply undercutting
the bank, a good cover of foam
on the eddy, caddis always, shifting
schools of dace. Still, once a year

I wade the riffle at its head, move
into the shades of the clay bank
and fish the run—a nymph
to an expected hatch, though nothing
has ever come of it, nor of a dun
cocked prettily in the drift line. Today,
the same. I lie in the sand

by the oxbow and watch, imagining how
one day my fly might ride
true in the feeding lane, and in a shimmer of spray
the river will burst and I'll be staring
into the ravenous power
I've always known
to be holding there. I know

of other spots like this one, where
in some fluid congress of the general dark
something heavy takes
secret breath, by reason of
its sheer bulk wary, and at pains
to conceal the breaking
of surfaces. Here lies in wait
what feeds by night, but only then.

Bullhead

Sprawled belly-down on the damp planks,
the breath squeezed in my chest,
I drift the worm into the pale
moon-shadow of the dock

and wait for the blunt emergence
of bullhead, his slow
surge to the bait, glint
of the small, mucusoid eye—
sluggish black spasm of flesh,

he bites, and I haul him out,
but he does not die at once.
Ugly among fishes, poisonous dorsal spine erect,
he endures, he swims in the air
for hours, scrabbles and grunts
in the bucket. A thousand times I've heard

that gross croak from the bucket.
Now it comes to memory from that peculiar sleeplessness
which loves those things which resemble

other things. Night after night
I have tried to breathe
the inappropriate air, wanted to cry out
into the blackness beyond
the dumb, immediate blackness

that I am about to die and cannot die,
but have made so dull a voice of the dull
connatural agony, I've writhed to it,
grunting aloud, the hook

of the breath snagged
in my gullet, the tongue
in my mouth like a worm.

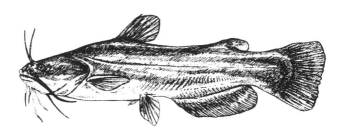

Muskrat

The sky opened itself
to the reedy smell of the lake,
the moon rode
in a parting of clouds
for fully a minute,
and I glanced out at the water
through the clusters of pale evening duns on the screen,
through the moon-lighted dazzle
of their wings, and saw

the fiery V-shape bearing out
into the shatter of light on the lake,
slow comet of small flesh
whiskery with grasses.

A small light of stars
in the opening clouds, room light
behind me—in that night without true fire,
everything cold, night deepening, the lake
deepening, the deepening clarity of flight
in the wing of the imago,

I raised my arm and room light flung
the long, articulated shadows of thumb and finger
out over the lake, out there, where
through the cold adaptive fires
of the cold stone of the fireless moon
the muskrat swam. It was enough

to frighten him, to make him dive,
frantically, smoothly webfoot down
through the rank blacknesses of lake, his fur
trailing light, his wake starry with bubbles,
his body light with the last terrified breath-taking. He dived
into the thickening muds of the lake,
and what remained, what I was left to see,
was the floating scatter of cattails,
and how the black field of the lake
closed on his small, inexplicable fire.

PART II

The North Branch

THE NORTH BRANCH

We took the train to Lakewood.
There'd been fires in the old days, swept
the North Branch country,
but over the years we fished there
most of the land recovered itself
in second-growth popple and wild
cherry, scrub maple
and birch. Blackberry
and raspberry bushes got thicker every year
in the clearings, and in the shadow
of this scrub, here and there, you saw

seedlings of hemlock from the few
remaining stands, even a few
white pine that came
from god knows where. And fern, may apple, winter-
green, coral mushrooms, *russula,*

and everywhere you looked
stood the charred stumps of the old pines,
some of them too big for the two of us
to join hands around. Made you wonder
what it must have been like

before the fires and lumbermen. It was
hard country
around that river,
killing frosts

by the middle of September, in October
snow began, lasted
six months, by the third week
of April you might see
a little grass again. When my brother
and I fished those rivers

we found a farmer let us sleep
in his hay barn, we'd pull together
a four-foot mound of hay
and sink into it, and get waked up
by the mice stirring in the hay,
and know by that it was daylight
and time to get up. No rats, thank god,
big pine snakes underneath the barn,
saw them lots of times
sunning themselves on stumps. Used to be

that river was something, read once
in the files of the old *Green Bay Advocate*
of a party took seven hundred
and eleven trout in three days
of fishing. This was

at the end of August, 1871. Another time
some years later four hundred
and sixteen fish that ran
a quarter pound to two and a half. Nothing
like that anymore, of course, and of course
that's why. But I tell you

it was still a beautiful stream,
the North Branch, in the upper reaches
wild, but lower down
a river for swans, maybe
forty feet wide, in places, and running deep
between the banks, and a powerful

current, so that even in the glides
it was punishing to wade
upstream, and then below the highway
it spread out in
a still water, but still

with lines of drift that went
past us quicker than we could wade
or walk the banks. We'd come
to the stream with the wet brush
in our faces, and sometimes we'd stand

on the meadow bank below
the oxbow and see
little grayish blobs of insect shapes
bobbing to the surface and fumbling

themselves airborne, and twenty feet out
the neb of a trout showing and gathering
one in, and then a hatch or spinner flight
filling the air, swallows by the dozen
hawking among them, cedar waxwings
coming out of the trees to take
one fly, and every square yard
of the stream with a feeding

trout. Black flies
could be bad, especially around

the pilings of the cattle bridges,
crawled down your collar, into
your ears, up your nose, your cuffs, bit
like a sunuvabitch, I used to think we'd maybe lose

a pound of meat apiece to them
some days. But we'd stay at it
no matter what, until almost sunset,
when the chill at last got to us,
and we'd come off the stream
shivering, bleeding, exultant.
In those days that was a river
where unless hot prairie winds were blowing in

from Kansas, or the Fox
had opened the reservation dam
and sent down a head of muddy water,
we felt we could take fish

somewhere along it—even
on the worst days we used to take
a lot of brookies in the riffles, small,
but by god they'd brighten the day!

Hatch

Another month
and the fly-making season
is on us, just barely time
before we're wader-deep
in May, and the Clyde runs clear again
and the bats begin to fly,
and by the end of the month

I'll be back in the meadows
where some years ago
near Decoration Day there came
a hatch of little gray flies with yellow
egg sacs, dense over
the river, and great

red-sided fishes wallowing
all around me, to which I passionately cast
all day with the right hand
until the right hand gave out, whereupon

I used the left and wore that out, too,
but never struck a fish—and didn't I have
a very bad moment when at last it occurred to me
they might be suckers, and struggled down

to the riffles at the tail
of the pool, and kicked some out,
and sure enough they were, big
five-pounders, striped bloody red

as a North Branch rainbow—since when,
the end of May and that hatch on,
I travel to some quiet place
where I figure trout
must be rising to it—nevertheless
can't help myself but look
more than twice at any
surfacing red sides.

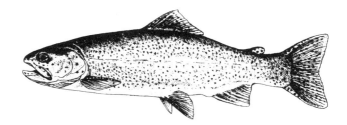

GREEN BAY FLIES

Two deep rivers ran
through the heart of town to the Bay,
and in March I watched the ice break up
and the big floes go tumbling, splintering
the piers, debarking the oaks and pines
along the banks four feet up their trunks.
In April, the first thunder
in six months, proclaiming
spring, and in July
up from the Bay, from beyond
Peet's Slough and Long Tail Point
and the marsh meadows blue
with sweet flag the hatch came,
a fly or two fluttering

to the street lights, then a few more, then
before you knew it
the mayflies of Green Bay would be swarming up
the Fox in huge rustling clouds half as wide
as the river, so many they darkened the arc lights
on the Blue Jays' field, covered
every window pane, clustered the screens, clogged
car radiators, covered your hat, your sleeves,
sometimes even brought traffic

to a halt. You could feel their wings
brushing your face with little breezes
that I swear were enough
to cool you down on a hot night, the air
adazzle with wings, and high

in the evening sky swallows
by the hundreds, cedar waxwings
darting out from the trees to meet a fly
just perfectly in mid flight, one second
this little fluttery dab of golden light,
then the flash and hover
of the bird, then

nothing,
like a flicked switch, the evening gone
minutely the darker for it.
If it had been raining
the streets and sidewalks in the morning
would be slippery with a green slime
of eggs, the flies having mistaken
the wet concrete for a surface
of live water. But nothing

like it anymore, the hatch
is over, probably
forever, the Bay a soup
of silt and sewage and sulfides
from the mills, not even clean
enough to swim in anymore. But back then,
those summer evenings—I can still
hear it, the sound
like a long train
way off in the distance,
a sort of humming rumble
wrought up by those millions,
billions, of delicate wings

that caught up every last scrap of light
left to the day in that last
half hour as night came down
and the street lamps
came on. I've never forgotten
how it was those years in July
the night stepping in, slow

and deliberate as a heron, the sky
softly darkening like it does
even now, evenings
in late summer, a smell
of lawns and dust and the steely
scent of the Bay drifting in, the air

still hot, but a growing softness
to everything—at such a time
you could surprise
yourself, catch sight of yourself
in a shop window, if the time
was right, and the mayflies
hadn't yet swarmed the glass, and depending
on how you wanted to look to yourself,
in such a light you'd look it.

A Fly Box

In those days when even the beaches
of Green Bay were clean enough
for swimming, the marshes
had muskrat houses and dogfish minnows
and snipe and nesting mallards,
and the wild blue iris that we called
sweet flag—in those days

we fished Queen of the Waters, Ginger Quill,
Coachman, Grizzly King, Brown
Hackle, Gray Hackle,
White Miller, maybe

a Parmacheene Belle from time
to time, Cowdung or Beaverkill,
but I favored
the Professor for tail fly, Silver Sedge
or Pink Lady for the dropper,
though nowadays

such dressings won't do,
the trout are all entomologists,
they don't find the idea
of a hatch of Professors
or Queen of the Waters especially
credible, and so

if you want a dressing
that seems to appeal to the large
modern trout, here's one, copied

from the Peshtigo's
Hexagenia limbata: *Wing*—dark
brown hair, bucktail, raccoon or mink, upright
and divided. *Tail*—hair fibers, as above.
Body—yellowish spun fur, ribbed
with bold spirals of brown. Rib the body
with brown hackle stems. *Hackle*—furnace, all this

on a 6 or 8 XL. With this dressing
I've had much luck across the years, even when
it went by the name
of *Dark Michigan Mayfly*.
Then, of course, there's the Red Quill,
Ephemerella subvaria, a great standby
throughout the early spring,
and at other times as well, and good
for several other flies common
in Vermont, one of them
an *Epeorus* of dark
complexion. *Leptophlebia*

cupida, this
is the Whirling Dun, although
you are likely to find it burdened
by almost any name, depending
on what fly the angler thinks
he's imitating. We have a writer
on the *Post* who called it last spring
The Barrington because
that happened to be the fly he was using
during the hatch, and he caught
a few fish, and so he wrote

"The sky was full of Barringtons." A difficult fly
to dress, for the wing
has lost its richness of slate,
and while almost transparent has
something of a brownish-bluish shade
lent it by the veins. As for the March Brown—
no comment needed. He won't often

be required, but when he is
you'll be sick if you haven't
a supply. *Stenonema vicarium,*
an admirable fly. If he
were an angler, he would be
wise, witty, clear-spoken, graceful, never

ponderous or opaque, never, or at least
not often, given
to ripe philosophizing,
forever observant, colorful, full of abhorrence
for the quaint and admiration
for the truly strong of character
and personality. Most authors say

you can substitute the March Brown for
the Gray Fox, when the gray *Stenonema*
is hatching, and *vice versa,* and no doubt
they are right, but I
have never tried it, and why should I, because
it's a great entertainment
to dress them both, no better waste
of time I can think of, and besides

if one is going in for imitation,
why do it half way? So I say
make up a dozen of the Gray Fox, and you'll be delighted
when you see the natural, abundant in Vermont,
Stenonema ithaca by name, dressed

in grayish mode, legs
handsomely banded dark
and light, very lively, quick

and independent of disposition,
with a personality that seems
developed, at least compared
with other mayflies. The Light Cahill is another fly

it's a pleasure to make, and lovely
to use when the eyes
are not as sharp as they used
to be, and even when they are, because
no matter, you can always see it.
And to it I owe

one three-pounder at the head
of Healey's Rapids, and the memory
of one of the same size lost
when the hook bent, and many smaller.
Black Gnat, Equinox Gnat

or Mosquito, these I employ
on the upper meadows of the Clyde, though seldom
on the Connecticut, where they have not
proved useful. The big idea
is to keep them small, no more
than two-thirds the size

the hook will accommodate, and even then
they'll look hopelessly too large. As for
the Blue Dun, an important fly

for the smaller hatches, I don't care
if you dress it as dark blue or iron blue,
but in either case keep it small. Sometimes

in the rain the trout will be slashing away
at the hatch of this fly,
and the gnats will be attacking
the little sails as they come down
the current, and you'll be able

to see the natural better
than the artificial, though if
you're wearing glasses,
you'll be hopelessly
up against it, because
in such weather the lens

fogs over the no doubt
already fogging eye, and I've seen
more than one angler gone thus blind
say the hell with it, clip off

his fly, sit down
discouraged on a rock,
and fish breaking

all over the pools!

White Miller

I'd watched him tie the fly, then catch
that fish, had seen it slurping away
in the big Clay Bank Pool on the South Branch
of the Oconto River, had tried for it myself,
slashing away with a floppy tip-dead castoff
South Bend nine-and-a-half footer someone
had dredged up for me from a far back corner
of the woodshed in Green Bay. I laid out

slashing casts, floated a soaked Brown Hackle
everywhere but over the big fish, for some reason failed
to put him down, finally gave up and yelled
for my uncle. I'll never forget
the wondrous calm
with which he looked things over. I've modeled
my aspirations to collectedness

on the way my uncle stood
that evening on the edge
of the Clay Bank Pool, on the South Branch
of the Oconto River not far
from Suring, light dimming, a late hatch

of something big and pale and vaporous
coming off the water like slight
coalescences of mist, mosquitoes
beginning to hum in my ear, a light breeze
in the overhanging branches of the white pines
on the far side of the stream, and just at the edge

of a midstream V in the current, over
and over again, that great, loud, leisurely insuck
of the big fish. I itched

for that fish, my mind was scoured clean
as a riffle by floods and freshets of desire. But Vince
just stood there, humming a little
to himself, finally said aloud

O.K., in the half-dark sure-fingered tied on
a fluttery-looking white thing
size of my thumb, and with his old-time
elbow-to-the-side-strictly-wrist-
and-forearm cast laid down that fly three feet above
and two inches to the right
of the rise ring, upon which the rainbow came
to the White Miller, and at that instant
arose in me on that day on the North Branch
in that fourteenth year
of what turned out to be
my life, this great, persistent yearning,

to possess that fly, to have it for my own, study it,
hold it in my hand, feel what vibrancy, what
radiance of blood it must have been
brought that big rainbow a foot
out of water, to hang blazing there
in what seemed to me
foreordination of fury!

LETTER

The eyes burn and the hands tremble
at your letter about the evening hatch
last Saturday on the big bend
of the Winooski, and it's
pure envy upsets me, no, regret
as much as envy, that I wasn't there
with you. What you tell me makes me wish

to change the subject, otherwise
I won't be able to get on
with what's left to me of my life. So

here goes, I've
kept busy, among other things been digging
into the history of the St. Joe valley,
and lately have made the acquaintance
of the Chevalier de La Salle,
likewise of Hennepin,
who, after nine months
on the lower Mississippi, and forced
to spend the winter at Michilimakinac,
thought to pass the dead time by preaching
on holy days. I remember

there was a stream not far
from Mackinac, I'd visit
it in July for a week, and every night I'd go down
to the river at six and fish till dark,
sometimes till after dark, and it
was gorgeous, standstill, one spot

did you for the night, you caught a trout
and waited five minutes till the others
started rising again, then went at it
again, or maybe walked
ten yards, in those days, though,

sometimes a little static for my tastes, I used
to like to move more. And I've discovered

that the Miami used to kill
as many as two hundred buffalo daily
near here, on the river plain
which is now the city dump, and that
a pioneer woman once killed a deer
with a pitchfork
in the Kankakee swamp. Most recently

I have spent one entire Holy Day
of Obligation killing,
skinning and pickling
a large French rabbit,
for *hasenpfeffer*. And what else? My old friend

Peaches Granfield
is dead, who used
to camp with me, we'd camp
at Idlewild to fish for trout and shoot
at bats. You might

have liked the latter—with a full
stomach and the supper dishes lying around and the bats
swooping out of the darkness of the spruces
to circle over the blaze, and Peaches

with a strong flashlight
cunningly held on one of them
I'd pepper away with the .410. Peaches
was a noble fellow, most perfectly
certain of his place in the world, in consequence
utterly insensitive. You may not know
he began as a butcher, but the trade

proved too dangerous
for a man like him, who could not talk
without waving his long arms around,
and one day he rammed a piece of chuck
into the grinder, and his hand
along with it, straight

into the hamburger, then retailing
at 18¢ a pound. Well, against

all reason I persist, keep

busy, can still
use my shop, handle the tools
quite as well as before, it seems, thank
God, or wing
a *Duchess* or a *Childers*
or a *Dirty Orange,* though when
I tire, I really sag, my legs

get cold and stiff, and even
the wood ticks don't seem to want me
anymore. I'd love
to have seen it, love

to have been there with you
with all those rainbows coming up
and eager for the fly, even if I had not
been able, as surely
I would not
have been, to fish. Mayflies,
against all reason, persist

on the St. Joe, a handsome
dark gray one lit on my hand
only yesterday, despite the fact

that this July the river
seems to be sweating, or at least
it's the color of sweat—you'll have
to imagine for yourself what I mean—lately,
though my eye for them persists,
the resemblances have begun
to resist my saying. This letter

is disorderly, I'm afraid, but things
are changing for me, therefore

for the world which over all these years
has accustomed itself
to being seen by me
in my particular way
and discovers it a grievous business
to have to reset itself, so that often
I wake up these days

in a confusion of recollection, maybe

on the North Branch, when I was young and just
beginning to fish, and could be on the water a week
and be alone, never see
another angler,

and there'd be wild rainbows rising, leaping, flashing
all over the pools, from bottom
to top, sometimes
the entire river seeming to go
green and crimson
with them, and I knew nothing
about the dry fly, though later

there came a couple of wild evenings
in the Oxbow when the March Brown
was on, and once on the Dugway Pool
with little olives, but mostly

it has been a slow
hard work, as we all
have come to know.

THE LITTLE BEAVER

The turbines at Johnson's Falls
up on the Peshtigo would open,
every morning at seven and the water
would come up three feet in thirty minutes, first
a few twigs and leaves, then a slight
muddying, and then before we knew it
we were having a hard time getting back
to shore, where the rocks and logs

we'd been sitting on an hour before
would be covered, only big V-shaped wrinkles
on the brown surface, and what had been a little riffle
would be a rapids filled with noise
and crazy water. At four

the slots would close, the water fall, and by five
the big river would be a series of clear runs
and riffles between pools. Where one tip of granite
had stuck up, now
a reef of bare rock and sand was drying
in the sun, a few trout would be making
neat swirls near the ledges of the far shore,
and along the banks where we walked
the sweet fern giving off smells
of verbena and sage. So midsummers

what with all the risings
and fallings, I used to give up
on the Peshtigo and seek out

the small rivers, like the Beaver, near Pound,
a little stream, two men fishing it
one man too many, yet
it yielded many a three-pounder,
though to look at it you had to wonder

how such a trout could find the room
to turn around. Try to get to it,
you had to crash brush so thick
you couldn't always get your arms free
to swat mosquitoes and black flies, and once

you came to the water's edge, you like as not
found yourself trapped in some alder hell,
black flies up your nose and in your ears, wood ticks
in your crotch, one foot
on a root above the water, the other
caught in a tangle behind you, or up
to the calf in a mudhole or quicksand, trout
darting away in every direction,
Little Beaver brookies,
spotted crimson in pale blue
halos, spotted lemon
and white, backs
moss-mottled-to-black, bellies
shaded off to a golden ivory,
fins striped orange and anthracite
and white—

Try wading it, you had to bend
double to keep under the arch
of the willows, and there would be

blockades of logs and roots to be stumbled
and scrambled over, and at every step you flushed out trout,

there in the brook like sardines. But finally
I had to give up
on that river, got a cramp

in my back one day, stooping
under the alders, had to crawl out through the swamp
on my hands and knees, was two hours
getting to my car, bad hurting all the way,
out of necessity took to fishing from a boat,
a real comedown I felt it,

going out with Fenske, who
isn't always too certain where he is
or what he's about, one time
when he looked up at the comet
fell over right on his back
in the marsh mud. A man

like Fenske's no good on a river
like the Little Beaver, goddam
pike fisherman, that's what he is,
hardly ever shaves, smells
worse than a skunk in heat,
drunkest man I ever saw,
if you were to give him two dollars
for telling the truth and twenty cents
for lying, he'd take the twenty cents

every time. He used to bring
two tons of gear along in his old GMC
when we went out, his feeling was
it was easier to take it all
than to have to figure out
what he needed. That was Fenske, he had what it took

to make a good pike fisherman—sorry,
Great Northern Pike fisherman. Fish & Game
and the Tourist Bureau people,
what they did was they took our sorry old jack pike
that nobody would carry through the streets
and want to be seen with, and give him
a brand new name, Great Northern Pike, and made
a million-dollar fish out of him. Wouldn't
of made fifty cents with *snake*, which is what
everybody called him when we was kids. Hell, that's what
I ought to do with carp, Great Copper Bass,
how's that? Make my goddam fortune, which God knows
I could use. One thing I've learned in an otherwise
pretty useless life, the name you give a thing
makes all the difference in the world. Oh, I loved that brook,

the Little Beaver, such beautiful
gliding water. When finally I'd break through to it
at the heart of that awful snarl
of swamp willow, cedar,
alder hell and mud, the world in thickets
between me and the road,
it would be trembling in the sun.

BIG WATER

My brother and I never caught
one of the big rainbows for which the Soo
was famous, though he hooked into something once
that smashed his rod with one run,
and left him swearing
like a sonuvabitch. Oh it was exciting
just to know they were there, the big fish,
and when the water was low

and the light was right you could look down
from the top of the dam at the head
of the river and see them, long
gray shapes lying easy in the water,
almost still, maybe once in a while
a little curl of a fin. One year
we heard of a local had been arrested
with a thirty-three pounder
that he'd speared. That kept us coming back
five years more at least, though between us
we caught exactly nothing, *half
of nothing apiece,* my brother said,
and we worked hard for it. We'd cross the locks
and fish all day in the tail race below

the powerhouse, edging out into
the heavy water to where
we didn't dare take another step, or turn

around even, and had to back
into shore over stones round and smooth
and slippery as you'd imagine
skull bones might be. Or we'd fish

from the spit of land beyond the tail race, in the rapids, bells
ringing behind us, horns bellowing and whistles screaming
from the ore carriers warped in to the big bollards
on the locks, men in foreign-looking caps
yelling up messages
to the crews on deck: *If you see Georgie McInnis*
in Duluth, tell him Oley
is working at the Soo. Other men

on the approaches to the locks
fished for whitefish with forty feet of line, and two
large mayflies on the hook, and you could look down
and see shining schools of fry, thirty yards
across, and suddenly
they'd melt away as a big trout
came cruising by only ten
or twelve feet down. It was good times, that's for sure,

when my brother and I
could get together at the Soo, big trout
on our minds, we'd be together at the Soo,
where we stayed at Mrs. Letourneau's Boarding House
every year in August for fourteen years
because it was cheap, and there was a tub
set on lion paws, and long enough
for a tall man to straighten out his legs, and deep enough
to bring the water to his chest—stayed there

in spite of the bugs. I remember
the first night there, I dreamed
I was covered with specks
of fire, woke up, there was a bug
working on me, I jumped up and pulled
the covers off the mattress, there they were,
half a dozen things big as potato bugs crawling up
the bed board, and I woke up my brother

in a panic, I said "There's bedbugs, the place
is crawling with bugs," but in the war he'd served
in India with the Brits, with kraits and cobras and bugs
that could swell your balls
to the size of cantaloupes, "What of it,
go to sleep!" he said. So what the hell, I went out
to the car and spent the night
in the back seat. Every year for fourteen years

my brother and I went back to work
the rapids, our heads aching with what
it would be like to hang into one
of those fish. Never did. Last year I went
back to the Soo alone, stayed one day, first time

in years, everything changed, my brother
dead, wife and daughter
dead, nobody talking

about big fish, the whitefish
long gone account of the lampreys, likewise
the lakers, everybody's mind
on something else or other, though lots

of guys out fishing on the docks
because of not much work,
and nothing much else to do, sitting there
waiting it out, bored and cold

in a sheeting rain that day, water pouring
off their hats and down their necks and into the sleeves
of their jackets every time they raised
their arms, and to top it off
the day I was there the turbines
were shut down, and the slots closed, the race
no more than a series of riffles and runs
between pools—though in the taverns

the proof was there, up on the walls behind the bars, over
  the mirrors,
in glass cases, there they were, the big fish, some of them
a little the worse for the years
they'd hung there, dusty, varnish peeling, paint
pretty garish in some cases, nevertheless for all
the bug-eyes, cracked and missing fins
there they were, mounts

of twelve- and fifteen-pound rainbows
came to the fly out there
in the rapids, the guides
straining at their poles trying to hold the canoes
upright and steady, the canoes
still pitching and rolling plenty, the sports
rolling out their heavy lines, the flies
floating down the feeding lanes
of that demented water,

and the great trout coming
to the fly, breaking water, suspending themselves
over the rapids, an outburst, a levitation
of high-leaping rainbows, striped scarlet, striped
cherry-red, green-
gilled, brilliant
in the ripe, sun-smelling day!

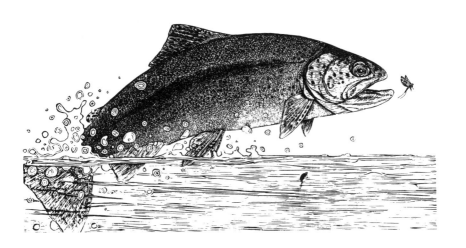

THUNDER RIVER

I used to love coming onto the dark pools
of the Thunder to find
a school of dace skittering
crazily along the surface, then everything

going still again, so that I knew
something big was at work, and it might pay me
to walk upstream and bait up a small hook with a tiny piece
of redworm and catch me a small dace and cut the tail off
and throw the rest back into the river where
it would turn and bump downstream along
the bottom giving back

little golden measures of light, then to thread
the chubtail onto a bigger hook and drift it
down into the pool and let it swing
in short silvery arcs, the sun meantime

rising higher, maybe a deerfly
buzzing in narrowing circles
around my head, the air
going heavy with the sweetness
of crushed ferns and warm hemlock.
But usually nothing

would happen, though once
in a while a big fish might flash
deep in the pool, or boil
at something I couldn't see, the thick back
porpoising, rise rings spreading
to splash the edges of the bank.

And always before I expected it
the sound of the woods would be rising
everywhere around me, the hour gone abruptly late
and dark having come on, wind
booming in the hemlocks
and behind me somewhere

where I'd never find them again
the runs and riffles of the Thunder
would come alive, the great pools
and oxbows flashing with big night-feeding

rainbows, swimming against the press
of the river, cavernously
gaping, flaring out ruffs
off scarlet gills, the water
storming about them, stony
in their throats, and the skin of the pools ashine
with schools of frenzied dace.
Exhausted, fly-bitten, muddy, hungry,

and sweating, I'd look up to see
nothing, no stars even, only the dark lock
and interlock of hemlocks—until
once on the road, I'd look up again and meet
the cool eye of the moon just
swum up from the deepest poolings of space,
for the rest of the night to poise itself directly
over wherever I might find myself
in my long walk home along County Z,
to hold itself steady and head-on above me
huge in the huge current of the sky.

Afterword

My first time on a trout stream was in the company of John Engels. Here is how I recollect it: John moved upstream, ahead of me, and frequently called to me, "Come up here! They're up here!" He was catching trout and putting them back. I was laboring to move in my new waders. Once when my new waders and I were not making a terrific commotion in the water, I could actually see fish holding steady in a clear, deep pool, but when I cast a fly more or less in their vicinity, they ignored it. I heard John shouting, "David! Come up here, they're up here!" Whenever I looked his way, I saw him playing a trout or carefully removing a trout from his hook and putting it back into the water. I moved eagerly toward him, but by the time I arrived at his spot, he had moved to another, farther upstream. He continued to call to me and to tell me that they were "Up here!" I got tired. I slipped on mossy stones a few times so that water went down inside the bib of my new waders—a fair portion of water. I swore to myself then that in spite of John's calling to me, I would stay in one place and merely practice my casting. That was when I snagged my line and broke off most of the leader that had taken me almost an hour to tie. The last time John shouted to me to "Come up here!" I responded to him in hastily chosen language. Then I sloshed my way out of the stream, and squooshed my way back along the bank. On the road, I peeled off my waders and poured a fair portion of water from each of its boots, then sat on the bumper of John's truck (which was locked) and smoked cigarettes while I waited for John to conclude his excellent afternoon of fishing.

This was around 1972, on a stretch of the White River near Royalton, Vermont, that is still as elegant a stream as it was when Edward Hopper painted it in 1937. Though I could hardly have had a less enticing introduction to the sport of fly fishing, I would, if John Engels called this morning to ask me, drive with him right back to the same spot and walk down to that water and try again to extract some trout from it. Since 1972, I have driven with him many miles and spent many hours with him on streams all over Vermont. When we're fishing together, John doesn't call instructions to me any more. One early evening on the Lamoille River, he even resisted advising me to give some line to the most significant trout I've ever hooked; thus he stood on the bank in silence and witnessed my line going limp when the trout snapped it. Now that is what I call a tactful mentor.

Nowadays, when we're on the stream, I don't try to follow John. His pace has never been one I could adjust to or imitate. I do take some time out to stand beside the stream and watch him "work." He covers a lot of water; he changes flies often; his casting is precise and efficient; he almost always catches trout; he almost always returns them to the stream. When John fishes with me, he also takes some time to stand streamside and watch me casting, but even when he sees me flailing the water, he doesn't criticize—he praises selectively, so that by what he has told me I've done well, I understand what I need to work on. As teacher and student in the high art of fly fishing for trout, John and I have made progress. I am honored to have this occasion to testify to his considerable ability both as a fisherman and a maker of poems about fishing. There are probably a few living fishermen who are more able than John, but so far as I know, among either the dead or the living, there are no more able makers of poems about fishing.

Around 1958 John Engels began publishing the poems that have won him recognition from the American literary community, including Guggenheim, Rockefeller, Fulbright, and National Endowment for the Arts fellowships. For nearly forty years, the great topics of literature—god, love, time, death, art, and the natural world—have had their way with this poet. When he has written about fishing, he has seen it in this context, as a lofty subject. As he has found fishing itself a noble endeavor. So it is perfectly natural and understandable that the great topics of literature have become the actual materials of Engels' fishing poems. Fishing and poetry are not hobbies; they are passions. Though they may seem to be dissimilar sorts of people, fishermen and poets are likely to understand one another, and these poems are the ultimately rewarding reading for fishermen.

When we read the poems of *Big Water*, we return to the beginning—to the origins of life, to the fundamental elements of human experience: water, air, stone, darkness, green leaves in golden light, coolness, and warmth. To step into a stream and cast a fly to a rising trout is to step back through thousands of years—or it is to step entirely out of time.

Paradoxically, this return to an elemental world opens up the most sophisticated levels of human perception. A complexity of experience becomes available. Our five senses acquire integrity and intensity; each sense cooperates intricately with the others to help us understand the immensely subtle processes of the natural world in which we participate when we cast flies to trout. What civilization has slyly taken away from us—we repossess through our experience on the stream. This richness of experience is what John Engels' poetry returns to us. To read these poems is to go back to some lost and essential part of ourselves. We find ourselves shaking our heads in the exaltation of contradictory but mutually felt responses: "I've never read anything like that!" and "I know that!"

"Foote Brook" ends this way:

... The brook was no more
than a minor brightness, yet its voice
was a powerful spasm of the night

and the large world everywhere
so bountiful an irregularity of surfaces

we could scarcely keep our feet

The poem gracefully balances the local and the universal. In this arrangement of exactly chosen words and lines is that giddiness a fisherman sometimes experiences on the water, of being in the presence of "the large world" by virtue of being so intensely connected to the "minor brightness" of the one spot of moving water where our waders have sought to anchor us.

As one who, thanks to John Engels, knows what it is to "scarcely keep [my] feet," I feel especially qualified to testify to the elevated level at which he practices the art of poetry. At the same time, his art is so vitally connected to human experience that when a reader is caught up in one of his poems, it doesn't feel like art at all. It feels real. The "Big Water" of the title poem is no longer in this world; we human beings have ruined it forever. The poem, however, has rescued it. These poems are as close to the actual experience of fishing the Big Water as it's possible to get.

—DAVID HUDDLE